MW00906876

THANK YOU FOR
CHOOSING US.
WE HOPE YOU ENJOY
COLORING
THIS BOOK.

Copyright ©2024 Shannon Voronova
All rights reserved. No part of this book may
be used, reproduced, or transmitted in any
form or means without written permission
from publisher.

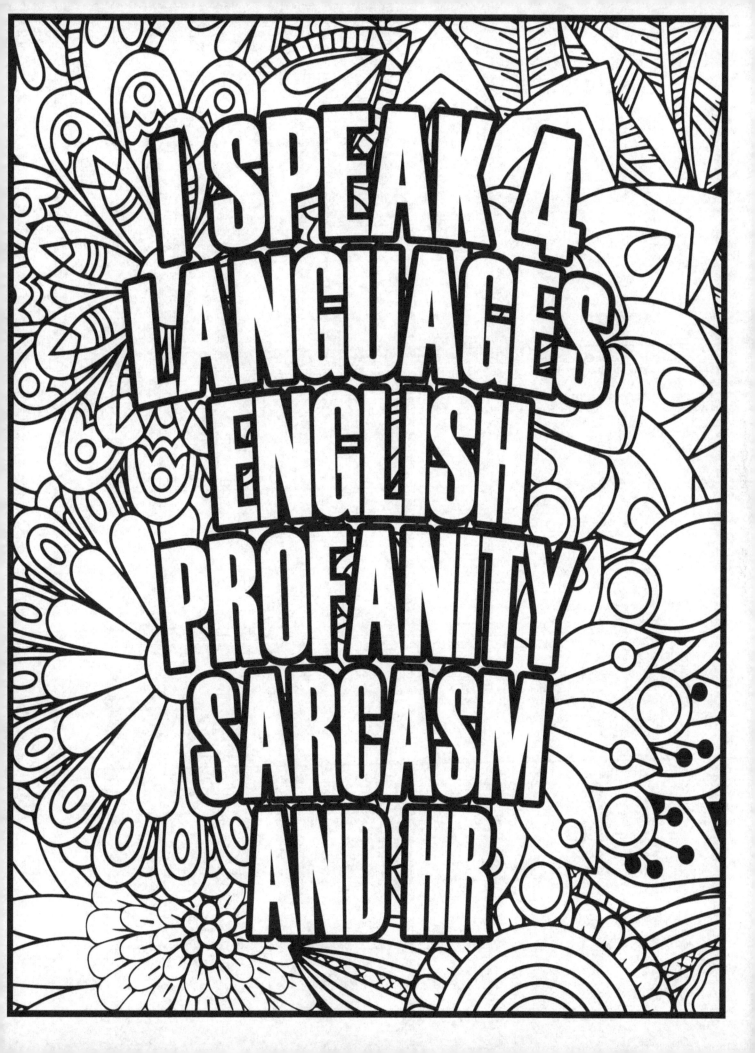

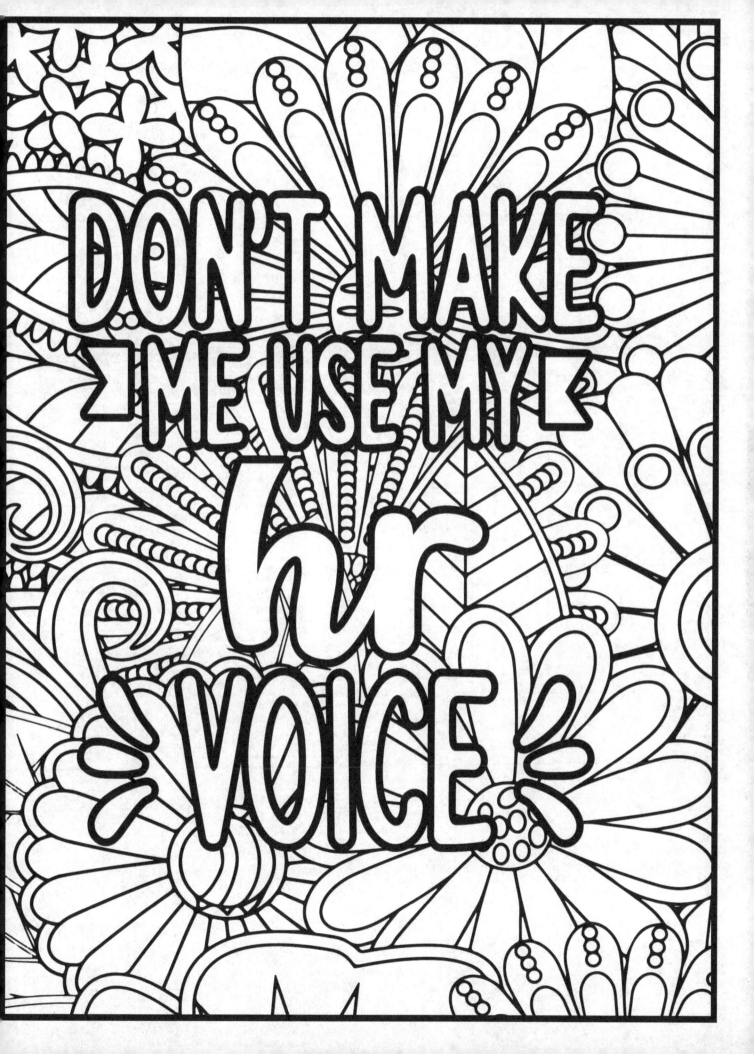

Made in United States
Troutdale, OR
12/05/2024

25907333R00031